ART WITH FOUND MATERIALS

John Lancaster

Consultant: Henry Pluckrose

Photography: Chris Fairclough

FRANKLIN WATTS
London/New York/Sydney/Toronto

Copyright © 1991
Franklin Watts

Franklin Watts
96-98 Leonard Street
London EC2A 4RH

Franklin Watts Australia
14 Mars Road
Lane Cove
NSW 2066

UK ISBN: 0 7496 0606 1

A CIP catalogue record
for this book is available
from the British Library

Design: K & Co

Editor: Jenny Wood

Typeset by Lineage Ltd,
Watford, England

Printed in Belgium

The author would like to
thank the following:
Henry Pluckrose for his
helpful assistance and
guidance, especially
during the exhausting
photographic session
when all the pictures
were taken; Chris
Fairclough, for his
excellent professional
skills with the camera.

Contents

This book describes activities which use the following:

Brushes (watercolour or hog hair)

Card (a variety of sizes cut from cardboard boxes which you can obtain from your local supermarket)

Cardboard boxes (several, to cut up as card; two or three to use as storage containers for your equipment and models; one to use as a spray box)

Chocolate boxes (or other small boxes to use as bases for models)

Cutting board (any flat off-cut of wood, hardboard or formica, larger than 10cm x 15cm)

Cutting knife (a Stanley knife or craft knife with a sharp blade)

Drill

Glue (strong adhesive such as UHU)

Jug (small, or small watering can)

Masking tape

Modelling clay

Natural forms (a selection – e.g., acorns, bark, dried grasses, fir cones, horse chestnuts, leaves, loofahs, nuts, sand, seed-heads, shells, sponges, stones and pebbles, twigs)

Paints – acrylic PVA
– coloured spray paint in a range of colours
– gold, bronze and/or silver spray paint
– household paint or lacquer

Ruler (30cm metal ruler)

Sandpaper

Saw (a tenon saw, junior hacksaw, fretsaw or coping saw with which to cut wooden bases to size)

Scissors

Tin lids (from discarded jam jars etc; plastic lids and plastic beakers can also be used as bases)

Tray (pottery or tin)

Water

Wood – short lengths of timber, e.g., 5cm x 5cm
– small off-cuts of hardboard or plywood

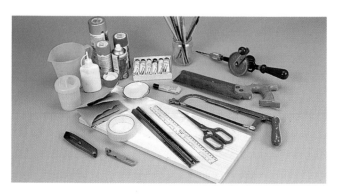

1 Some of the equipment you will need when making the sculptures in this book.

In this book you will be shown how to design and construct simple three-dimensional models. Such models are called sculptures.

If this is the first time you are attempting this kind of art work, read through each section carefully. By following the instructions and ideas, you will soon find that you are able to produce small, worthwhile sculptures.

You should be able to find the natural materials listed without difficulty, and at no cost. Your biggest expense will be on spray paint and glue, but use oddments of household paints to colour your sculptures if necessary.

Some hints

Always wear a smock, apron or old shirt to protect your clothes when you are working. Work at a bench, a table covered with strong paper or plastic, or on an area of floor protected by a sheet of hardboard, plastic, or brown wrapping paper.

From time to time a sculptor will look at the piece he or she is making, viewing it from the front and the back as well as from each side. These are vital stages, because they allow the sculptor to watch the progress of his or her sculpture from every possible angle. Do the same thing yourself. It will help you keep the proportions of each sculpture right and therefore allow the sculpture to grow well as a "designed" object.

Thinking in this way demands what are called "building and constructing" skills. The more you work, and the more critical you are of what you do, the more these skills will develop.

Do a drawing of each sculpture before you start, showing what you intend the finished sculpture to look like. Do a second drawing once the sculpture is complete. Compare the two drawings.

When cutting wood, card, twigs or other materials with a saw or sharp knife, take great care. Always work on your cutting board. Never point the knife at anyone. Never cut towards your body. Put the knife in a safe place after use, and replace the blade cover.

The first thing to do is go for a nature walk with a parent or friend and look for a range of natural forms. You should be able to find these in a garden or local park, in hedgerows or at the seaside. Take care not to damage any trees, shrubs, plants or fences. Take a suitable container (e.g., a plastic carrier bag) with you in which to carry back your finds.

Some natural forms for you to find

Some of the items on this list will be used for the activities suggested in this book. Collect these, but look around for others not on the list as well.

Dried ferns	Pieces of bark
Fir cones	Sand
Horse chestnuts	Shells
Leaves	Small stones
Nuts	Sponges
Pebbles	Twigs

1 A selection of natural forms.

Each sculpture you make will require a firm base on which to stand. Although various sizes of bases are suggested throughout the book, you can vary these depending upon the kinds of materials you use.

Prepare some bases in advance of making your sculptures. Here are some ideas.

1 Saw two or three wooden bases from a length of timber and smooth them with sandpaper.

2 Cut some pieces of hardboard or plywood, and sandpaper these to give a smooth, even surface.

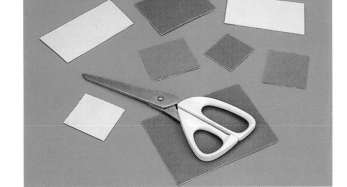

3 Cut a number of squares from thick card.

4 Collect a few small cardboard boxes.

5 Look around for other objects such as tin lids and small plastic beakers which could be used as bases.

6 Colour some of your bases.

Many natural forms come into being through natural growth or the effects of weathering. They are like beautiful sculptures, and are often rich in colour, pattern and texture. These features combine with the shape of a form to create something which is pleasing to look at.

You will need a collection of different natural forms, a selection of wooden bases and/or containers on and in which to display your natural forms, and glue.

1 Select a natural form and display it on a polished wooden base. This rock fell from crumbling cliffs into the sea below. It was turned into a piece of natural sculpture by the eroding effects of sea water and sand grinding out holes in its surface.

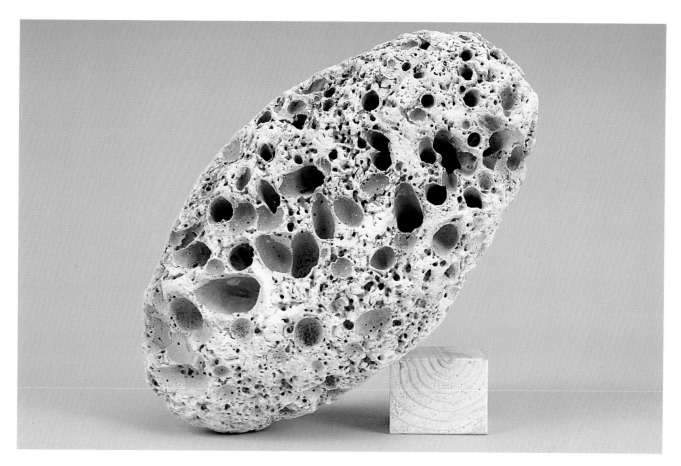

2 Pick up and handle the natural form you are working with before you decide on the base or container on or in which you are going to display it. Look at its colour and pattern, and feel its texture.

3 Sometimes a base is not required, and you can place your selected natural form on a bare surface. Do you know what this object is? It is tumbleweed from a prairie in North America, and is hard and spiky to touch.

4 Try grouping similar natural forms together.

5 Try grouping different natural forms together. Those which have similar or complementary shapes, colours and patterns often seem to blend well. You may have to glue the natural forms in position.

6 A finished "sculptural piece".

7 A simple arrangement of different natural forms.

Small, grotesquely-formed or gnarled twigs are interesting natural sculptures. They can be displayed on a base, or as a mobile sculpture suspended from a ceiling or beam by thin nylon thread. Display them singly or in groups of two or three.

You will need a gnarled twig, paints and paintbrushes.

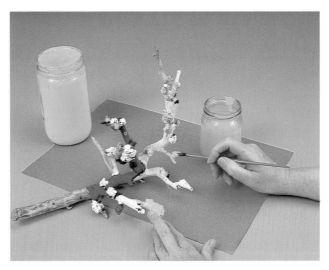

1 Some twigs look best painted in only one colour. Others benefit from being painted in two or more colours as this gives greater emphasis to their twisted shapes.

2 A finished twig sculpture.

A linear sculpture

Linear sculptures use simple lines to create an effect. You will need a strong wooden base, some dried stalks or twigs, glue, fir cones, paints and paintbrushes. Make the base for this standing sculpture by sawing a square piece from the end of a length of timber and smoothing it with fine sandpaper.

1 Cut or break off six lengths of stalks or twigs. These can range from approximately 25cm-35cm.

2 Cut or break off some shorter lengths, ranging from approximately 10cm-20cm. Glue a number of these shorter pieces across two of the longer pieces, to make a ladder-like construction. Make two more "ladders" from the remaining pieces of stalk or twig. Allow the glue to harden.

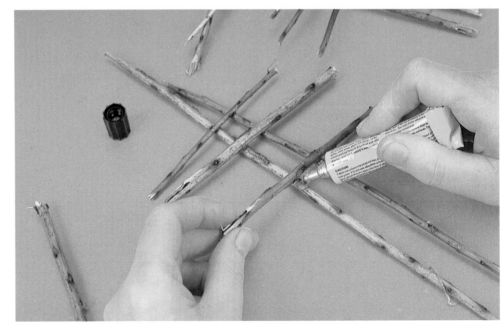

3 Glue the three "ladders" on to the wooden base, each one on a different side. Allow the glue to harden.

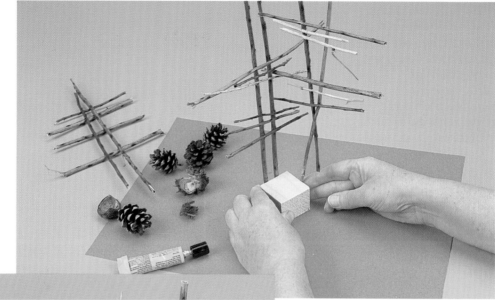

4 Decorate the top of the wooden base with fir cones or other appropriate natural forms.

5 The finished linear sculpture. Colour the sculpture by painting the stalks or twigs in three different colours, or by spraying the whole model with gold, silver or bronze paint.

6 Make a different type of linear sculpture by gluing a short length of painted cardboard tube on top of a painted base. Lay a ladder of twigs over the tube and glue it firmly in position. This sculpture can be free-standing or mounted on a wall.

Late summer and autumn are good times to collect seed-heads, nuts, acorns and fir cones. You will often find them lying on the ground around the bases of many different kinds of shrubs and trees. If you use such natural forms imaginatively you will produce some interesting sculptural models.

Seed-head sculptures

You will need a selection of seed-heads and horse-chestnut shells, wooden bases, glue, paints and paintbrushes.

1 Glue a half-opened horse-chestnut shell on to a small wooden base. Hold it in place until the glue hardens. Add more horse-chestnut shells, arranging them in such a way that you produce a standing model.

2 The horse-chestnut shells in this sculpture were twisted to one side as they were stuck together. This has produced an interesting shape. When the sculpture was finished it was painted yellow. Do you think this makes the sculpture more interesting, or are the shells more attractive left in their natural state?

3 A close-up of part of a horse-chestnut shell sculpture.

4 Two small models made from seed-heads.

An acorn sculpture

To make this sculpture you will need a wooden block (about 14cm long) to use as a base, some large acorns, glue, a fir cone, and seeds or pieces of dried grass.

1 Glue the first acorn on to the top of the base.

2 Add more acorns, arranging these to form a pattern.

3 When the acorns are secure, stand the wooden block upright. Complete the sculpture by adding a fir cone to the top.

4 The finished
sculpture.

5 Give the surface of your wooden base a more interesting texture by gluing seeds or pieces of dried grass on to it.

6 The base of this acorn sculpture has two textured sides.

7 Here, horse chestnuts – commonly called "conkers" – are being used to make a relief sculpture.

Two fir-cone sculptures

You will need two wooden bases, fir cones, glue, spray paint, a large cardboard box, a drill, and a twig between 12cm and 20cm in length.

1 For the first sculpture, glue a row of cones on to a wooden base. Decide for yourself on the length of the base.

2 Position the last fir cone at a different angle from the others, to give variety to your sculpture.

3 When the glue has set, colour your sculpture with spray paint. Make a spray box from a large cardboard box and place your sculpture inside, to protect you and your work area.

4 The finished
sculpture.

5 The second sculpture is more difficult to make. Begin by preparing a painted wooden base. Drill a hole in the top face of the base.

6 Glue five or six fir cones to the twig.

7 Position the fir cones on different sides of the twig, for variety.

8 Allow the glue to set, then slot the twig into the hole on the base. Secure the twig in this position with a dab of glue.

9 Glue two or three fir cones together to form a small group.

10 Arrange a number of these fir-cone groups around the upright twig on the base. Glue them securely into position.

11 The finished sculpture. Two of the fir cones have been coloured red, for effect.

Using sponges and loofahs

Sponges and loofahs are found in the sea in some parts of the world. If you go to such places on holiday, then you may discover one or two on the beach. On the other hand, you may have an old sponge or loofah at home that you can use.

These natural forms are full of three-dimensional holes and textures. They are interesting to look at and to touch. If you squeeze a dry sponge it will feel firm. Do the same when it is wet, and it will feel soft and "spongy". A loofah feels different. It is scratchy, and harder than a sponge.

You will need an old sponge or loofah, a saw or craft knife, glue and a base.

1 Use the saw or craft knife to cut your sponge or loofah into small pieces. Make sure the pieces are dry before you start work on your sculpture.

2 Glue the pieces on to the base you have chosen.

3 Arrange the pieces in an interesting pattern.

Try spray-painting the small pieces of sponge or loofah before you arrange them on the base. Paint two pieces in gold, two in red, and the rest in a colour of your choice.

Use different types of bases for your sponge or loofah sculptures. Try a tin lid, a plastic lid or an upturned plastic pot instead of wood.

4 In the unpainted sculpture shown here, cuts were made into a fairly large piece of loofah. The loofah was then opened out and glued on to a painted wooden base. Another small piece of loofah, cut in a different way, was then positioned in the centre. Its form contrasts nicely with the main loofah piece.

Now that you have made a number of sculptures, here are some other ideas for you to try.

A **sand-tray water erosion** sculpture

You will need a large tray, a short length of wood, stones and pebbles, sand, a piece of bark or one or two twigs, a jug or small watering can, and water. The tray shown in the photographs is a pottery one. A tin tray will do just as well, or you can make your own from a piece of hardboard or plywood approximately 60cm x 30cm with a wooden lip (2cm deep) all round.

1 Place the tray on the ground, on a solid concrete floor or on an area of floor covered with a plastic sheet. Raise one end of the tray between 2cm and 4cm away from the surface by placing a short length of wood underneath. Use pebbles or small stones instead of wood, if necessary.

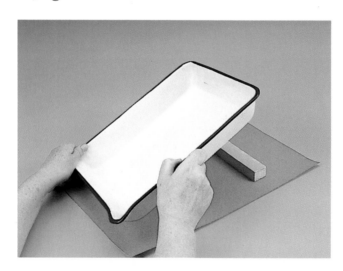

2 Scoop some sand into the tray.

3 Form the sand into small hills, valleys and flat areas. Try to make your sand-tray look like a landscape.

4 Lay some pebbles and stones on the sand then add the piece of bark or the twigs to create the effect of fallen tree trunks.

Rain showers erode our own landscapes over many weeks, months and even years. Look around to see the effects of rain and wind upon the fields, hills or coastal areas near where you live.

How does your own "eroded landscape" compare with erosion in the outside world?

5 When you have created your landscape, gently dribble some water on to it. Using the jug or small watering can will help you control the flow of water. Make sure the water does not run out of the lower end of the tray, and quickly mop up any water which does escape.

6 Repeat this process from time to time over a period of three or four days. Observe what happens to the sand in the tray and how the water affects your small landscape. Keep a notebook with sketches, maps, photographs and written notes about what happens.

Shells

When you go to the seaside, make a collection of shells, large and small. Sort them out carefully when you return home.

1 Make a "relief" sculpture by arranging shells in straight lines or in circles on a strong base of plywood or thick card 20cm x 20cm.

2 Using a strong adhesive, cover the four sides of a strong cube (either wood or card) with small shells. When the shells are attached securely, add more to the top of the cube.

3 Glue small shells all over an inverted plastic beaker or yoghurt carton. Spray your finished sculpture with gold, silver or coloured paint.

7 A collection of shells.

Clay models

The models in pictures **8**, **9** and **10** were made with clay. One was based on seed-heads, another on a pebble. Which one was based on a mushroom?

Using modelling clay, make one or two models yourself. Use a small stone, shell or piece of loofah to help inspire what you do.

8 A clay model.

9 A clay model.

10 A clay model.

Bark

Different species of tree have barks which vary in pattern and texture. Some are smooth, while others have rough surfaces. Look for some pieces of bark which have fallen away from old tree trunks or branches. These may be rough and deeply etched.

ON NO ACCOUNT SHOULD YOU DAMAGE TREES TO OBTAIN BARK.

Think of ways of using bark to make interesting sculptures. You can keep the pieces of bark whole, or break them into smaller portions.

11 A tree bark sculpture.

Now have fun thinking up ideas of your own.

Most of the materials mentioned in this book are easy to obtain. Many of them – particularly the various kinds of natural materials – can be collected in the local environment near to where you live. If you are lucky enough to have a garden, you can search in it for wood, twigs and other natural materials. If you live in the country, you will have hedgerows, fields and woods in which to look. Those who live in towns can often go into a park for their finds.

Materials such as wood can be bought in local shops or in DIY stores. Paints, paintbrushes, spray paints, crayons and inks may be obtained in most stationers or in artists' materials shops.

Larger quantities of materials, as well as certain items of equipment, can be ordered through suppliers of artists' materials. The following suppliers are very helpful:

E J ARNOLD & SONS, Parkside, Dewsbury Road, Leeds LS11 5TD

MARGROS LTD, 182 Drury Lane, London WC2

WINSOR & NEWTON LTD, 51 Rathbone Place, London W1

It may be difficult to find books concerned with making art from found materials. Visit your local library and ask whether they have any books concerned with sculpture, so that you can see what artists such as Henry Moore and Barbara Hepworth created. Also ask to see books concerned with natural scenery and natural forms – rocks, bones, shells, cliffs, sand patterns, etc. Take a little time to look for photographs of these things in magazines and newspapers. If you cut them out you will soon have a useful collection of resource material to refer to. Such a collection will be invaluable as you begin to try to develop your own ideas.

PRINTED IN BELGIUM BY
proost
INTERNATIONAL BOOK PRODUCTION